A GUIDE TO
ESSAY WRITING
PRODUCING THE IDEAL ESSAY

Rita Pullen

Straightforward Publishing
www.straightforwardco.co.uk

Straightforward Guides
Brighton BN2 4EG

ISBN 184716 042 5
ISBN 13: 978184716 042 3

Printed by Biddles Ltd Kings Lynn Norfolk

Cover design by Bookworks Islington

ACKNOWLEDGEMENTS

Thanks to The University of Essex for allowing me to use the essay titles on pages 39, 40 and 117, marked with an asterisk (*), which were set during my period as an undergraduate and also to all those individual lecturers, teachers and students who gave so freely of their support, encouragement and suggestions. Thanks also to Malcolm for his patience.

RP

CONTENTS:

INTRODUCTION

The skills required for essay writing are the same as those required for employment. The ability to communicate fluently and clearly in writing is essential in letters, reports, press releases and many other business documents. This book is intended for those who are starting to write formal, academic essays and for those who would like to improve the standard of their work.

Embarking on higher level courses, including A-levels, degrees and vocational training courses, can be daunting to those with little experience of essay writing, or for those who lack confidence, but this book will provide some basic advice and guidance which will enable the reader to gain a better understanding of what is expected of her or him.

Schools, universities and colleges will differ slightly in their requirements, as will individual tutors within those establishments, but all will be looking for concise, focused and well researched essays. This book will help you to achieve a high standard in your written work.

When you are asked to write an essay, you are being asked to provide an argument which you can explain and justify, one which (depending on the title provided) supports, criticises, explains or discusses one or more points. Your argument or arguments must be based on your research and must be:

- objective: supported by evidence and not influenced by your own personal prejudices or emotions

- logical: consistent and clearly reasoned on the basis of the evidence to hand

- precise: well-defined and unambiguous

Your essay should present your arguments in a well-organised way and show that you have engaged with the course, researched your subject thoroughly and analysed it critically.

There are several stages to essay writing and, in an ideal world, you would have plenty of time to devote to each of them but, in reality, they will need to overlap to a certain extent, depending on the time you have and the availability of resources. This book will guide you through the stages and offer advice on some of the best ways to tackle them.

Chapter 1

Working Constructively

There are several steps to writing an essay. You will need to:

- choose and think about your essay title

- collect material for your essay – library books, course books, newspaper/journal or magazine articles, hand-outs, lecture notes etc.

- write a brief essay plan incorporating your initial ideas for essay content

- write your first draft

- edit and correct your draft (with constant reference to the essay title and word limit)

- carry out a final check to ensure that everything is as you want it to be (including presentation) then print/write your essay, collate and submit it

However, before you even start to think about your essay title, you will be attending lectures and classes and you need to ensure that you are benefiting as much as possible from your study time. This first chapter will help you think about the best way to work.

i.   Taking notes

Every student will have her or his own way of assimilating the information given in a lecture. Some will merely sit and listen – and appear to absorb (and recall) information without difficulty. Others will frantically take notes almost verbatim, in rapidly scribbled long-hand or even in shorthand. In between those extremes there are as many ways of making the most of a lecture as there are students in attendance – and you need to decide the best way for you.

You might decide on straightforward written notes, taking down important points and ensuring that your notes represent the substance of the lecture. You might prefer the more visually stimulating reminders provided by flow-chart (or "mind-map") notes, where the main topic of the lecture forms the central hub of your notes and the sub-themes are linked to this by arrows, loops or lines (see Figure 1 at the end of this section). You might even like to take a tape-recording of a lecture (if this is allowed by your establishment - and you should ask before assuming that it is acceptable to take a recording machine into a lecture with you). Some universities have a recording system allowing students to collect tapes of a lecture, for a small fee, from a technician.

Writing notes (or using a flow-chart or other written method) is an active way of engaging with the lecture and, while a tape-recording of a lecture will give you a long-lasting record of what was actually said, this method of "note-taking" is not as helpful as it is convenient.

Each system has advantages and disadvantages but, whichever method you choose to help you remember your lectures, do keep your notes in order, with the title of the lecture, the name of the lecturer and the date.

Clearly, if you have been unable to attend a lecture, through ill health or for some other genuine reason, then a recording is the next best thing to attendance. However, if you choose to tape record a lecture, rather than taking notes, then remember that it is easy to "drift off" and lose concentration during an hour-long lecture in a warm lecture theatre, especially if you are tired. Knowing that the lecture is being taped can remove any incentive at all actually to listen to what is being said. You will, of course, have your tape to listen to again – but it is very difficult to summon the energy and the inclination to listen to the whole lecture and concentrate if you have dozed through it once already. You might find it difficult to concentrate again – and then you will have wasted *two* hours and still not really "listened" to the lecture.

The physical process of taking notes reinforces the content of the lecture. However, unless your notes are very clear and reasonably coherent, it is a good idea to write (or type) them up as soon as you can after a lecture, if you have the time. This exercise serves several purposes:

- it is more likely that you will be able to read, and rewrite, your notes shortly after you have taken them than if you leave them "as taken" and try to decipher them later in the term. We take notes to remind us of the content of a lecture. The exercise is rendered pointless if notes are illegible or incomprehensible.

- writing-up notes again will reinforce, and help you to remember, what the lecturer said.

- If there was anything in the lecture which was not clear, it is always easier to approach a lecturer for clarification shortly after the lecture, rather than going to her or him at the end of Week 10 and saying "I didn't understand what you meant in the lecture in Week 2". Writing up your notes will help you to identify any points which need clarification.

If you do not have time to write or type-up your notes, you should, at least, read through them after the lecture to see that they make sense. Always keep notes from a lecture stapled together, dated and with a note of the lecturer's name and the title of the lecture.

Always try to be alert and looking for material which might be useful in essay writing. A quote[1] from a radio or television programme (providing it is properly referenced) could be used

---

[1] It is common, when discussing essays with tutors and other students, to use the more informal "quote" when we mean "quotation". In this book, I will use the word which is familiar to us all and will refer to "quotes".

to make, or challenge, a point in your essay and, if you get into the habit of keeping any appropriate newspaper articles (noting the name of the newspaper and the date) these can be used to provide an up-to-the minute perspective on your subject.

At the very least, any relevant reading, viewing or listening will give you a deeper understanding of your study subject.

<u>Now read the key points overleaf.</u>

<u>TAKING NOTES – key points:</u>

- Take your notes in the way *you* find most useful.

- Always read through your notes after a lecture. If there is anything you do not understand – ASK.

- Organise your notes and keep them together – labelled and dated.

- Look out for material for your essay at all times.

****

ii. Choosing your essay title and collecting material

You might not be given a choice of essay titles to choose from but, if you are, please do not worry if your first reaction to the list is "I can't do this". Everybody has thought that at some time or other. Try to remember that you are in your class, or you have been given a place on your course, because you *can* cope with the work and the academic demands. You did not just walk in off the street. Your college, school or university has accepted you onto this course because you are capable of completing it successfully.

You should be given a "word limit" for your essays at the same time as you are given the titles. If you have not been given this information, then ask for it straight away. It is usually acceptable for the word count of an essay to be up to 10% higher or lower than the word limit but do not take this for granted. Again, ask if you are not sure.

If the essay titles fill you with dread, you will not be the only one feeling this way. There will be some people, flourishing the list of titles, saying "Easy, I can do this". Remember – they are probably trying to convince themselves as well as convince you. A few students will be undaunted by the prospect of writing an essay on a subject which is new to them and having to submit it for assessment to a lecturer they do not know - but those people will be in a very small minority.

You will probably need to give your essay title some thought to ensure that you really understand what it means and what your tutor is looking for. Look up key words in a dictionary or course book if you are in any doubt as to their meaning. If you have friends among the other students, now is the time to draw on the support they will be able to give you, and that you will be able to give them. Discussing the essay titles will help clarify what is needed and help you to start thinking more clearly around the subject.

If you do not have anyone else with whom to discuss things, DO NOT PANIC. Look at the titles calmly and start the "choosing" process by being realistic. If you have doubts about whether you really understand the title of the essay, check that you know what the keywords mean. If there is a special dictionary for your subject, this will prove invaluable; otherwise, simple definitions in a basic course book should help you.

When selecting a title from the list, try to choose to write an essay on a subject which really interests you. This will enable you to engage with the subject and write with more feeling. If you found all the lectures fascinating, absorbing and enlightening – and you have organised, legible notes from all of them, then you are lucky indeed and can probably choose any title. However, if this is not the case and none of the titles is immediately appealing, then try to think back to the lecture(s) appropriate to each title. Did you find one of them more interesting than the others? Did one of them just engage you slightly more than the others? Did you feel that you understood one more than the others? Do you feel that you have better notes from one particular lecture than you have for the others?

All the titles will be manageable but you will find that at least one of them will be more appealing to you than the rest of the list and, with a little thought, you will be able to identify it.

Collecting material

From now on, if you have not already developed this habit, you should carry a pad and pen with you at all times. You will have brilliant ideas about your essay content but probably never at a convenient time. If you can always jot down your flashes of inspiration – a phrase, an opening sentence, a way of explaining something - then you will be able to use them when you settle down to start writing.

When you have decided which essay to write try to get to the library as soon as you can. Remember, you will not be the only student looking for books relevant to your chosen essay title. It should not be necessary for you to spend a great deal of money on books. Your main course books will be a good place to start your research – they will give a concise interpretation of theories and they will also refer to the primary texts which will enable you to further your research on the topic. Primary texts are usually the original work of a particular author or other works, written at the same time; secondary texts are subsequent works (such as anthologies) which look at the original text and analyse or criticise it, or use it as a basis for further theorising.

Do remember to make a note of reference material as you identify quotes, regardless of whether they are from a primary or a secondary source. This is especially important if you are working in the library and copying quotes from journals, reference books or "short loan" items but it is a useful habit to get into for every quote you use. If you use a quote without referencing it properly, you could be accused of plagiarism. If you get into the habit of writing down referencing details for each quote you use, or think you might use, then this will never be a problem.

When you find a good quote, it is likely that you will be so pleased with it that you think you will always remember who said it and which book it came from. You probably will not. There will be more about referencing and plagiarism later in this chapter but, for now, it is vital that you jot down all the relevant information for *every* quote you think you might use, i.e. author, date of publication, source, volume/issue number or edition (if appropriate) and place of publication/publisher. It is also useful to write the page number of the quote. While this will not necessarily be considered essential by your tutors, it will help you trace the reference when you come to revise for exams.

At university or college you will have been given book lists for lectures and course work. These books will investigate your subject in more depth and there should be several copies of the most useful texts available in your university or college library. If all the shelf copies have been borrowed, then you should be able to find a specific book in the "short loan" section of the library. If this is your only option, then you will have to be very focused with your reading and have a photocopy card to hand so that you can copy essential pages. Remember to write on your photocopies all the information you will need about the book for referencing purposes.

A search of the library computer system using keywords should also lead you to interesting books which might give a different perspective on the topic about which you have chosen to write. Always read as much as you can around your subject. Even a theory which has been discredited or superseded can help you to get a broader view of your subject and set it into context more easily.

If you think you will need to refer frequently to a text then a visit to a second-hand bookshop might be fruitful. Find out if your student union has such a shop and whether it is open for usual shop hours, or just staffed at certain times or on certain days. The most widely used books on all the subjects taught in your department will find their way there and, if you buy one, you can always re-sell it when you have finished with it.

You will have easy access to your school, college or university library but the public library is also a very useful resource. The books in each library in a county might not be as specialised but the catalogue will be vast and you can request specific books from other libraries via the computerised system. It is likely that you will be able to access your county library catalogue on-line – either from the library website or via the website for the county council – this means that you can place an order for a book without visiting the library and you will be notified by e-mail (or text if you so choose) when the book is ready for collection.

This is a good time to say that if you still really feel that you have problems or insurmountable difficulties with the course or with your essay, then you should speak to a member of staff. Your college or university will have a Student Support Officer who will help you to sort things out, or you could see your personal tutor or the subject lecturer.

If your tutors have special times to see students, then go during those periods. If they do not, then try to make an appointment or, at least, pick a time when your tutor does not have to rush off to give a lecture and ask when would be a convenient time to discuss your problems.

Have a clear idea of what you want to say and try to be as specific as possible. You will definitely not be the first student to need a bit of assistance but tutors will need more information than "I can't do this" if they are going to be able to offer constructive advice. If you can be more precise, for instance: "I don't understand the essay title. Can you clarify this point for me, please?" or "I think the essay title refers to xyz, am I on the right lines here?" then the person you approach will be able to focus on your question and give you useful advice.

If you need information about the practicalities of the course then the administrative staff in your departmental office will be able to give you informal, friendly help and a listening ear.

If you have a personal problem which you think is affecting your ability to cope with the course, then there will be a student counsellor who will be able to help. It must be stressed that all of these people will treat what you tell them with the utmost confidence and they will not share information unless you have given your permission or unless it will affect other people.

Now read the key points overleaf.

<u>CHOOSING YOUR ESSAY TITLE – key points:</u>

- Choose your essay title with care.

- Make sure you understand what is expected of you.

- Always take full referencing information with your quotes.

- If you have any worries – talk to someone.

****

iii.   Choosing when and where to work

If you are writing this essay in familiar surroundings, with your usual support network available, then there is no need to change anything that has led to success in the past. However, if you are writing your first essay in a different environment and in completely different circumstances from those you are used to, then you need to think about making things as comfortable as possible for yourself and writing in a place and at a time which will enable you to produce your best work. You will need to be disciplined about keeping up with your workload but this will be easier if you can arrange things so that you are working comfortably and constructively rather than just sitting, blinded by panic, producing nothing very worthwhile.

When?

Make sure you know all your essay deadlines and exactly what has to be submitted on which date. With practice, you will know how long it is likely to take you to research, draft, write and submit a good piece of work but, until then, make sure you give yourself enough time to work in a way that suits you. Remember, everyone works in a different way. It does not matter how other people work, whether it is more quickly than you or more slowly. You must find the way that is right for you.

Perhaps you know already at what time of the day or night you work best? Are you a night owl, producing your very best work when everyone else is either in bed or out for the night? Do you like to rise early and study before anyone else is even up?

Perhaps you work better in short bursts – half an hour or so of concentrated effort several times a day? Or do you manage to give your best when the pressure is on and you are completely focused? Only you can decide at what time you will work best. Perhaps you can focus and write at any time of the day or night – if so, you are very lucky. There is only one rule – DO NOT WASTE YOUR TIME. There is no point in sitting for hours on end, twiddling your thumbs and producing nothing but anxiety. Obviously it is not a good idea to make this rule an excuse for doing nothing but you do have to exercise enough discipline, and be mature enough, to recognise when you are time wasting and either knuckle down to some *real* work or do something else completely for a while and then return, refreshed, to your essay. Two hours of concentrated, focused effort is more productive than a whole day of shilly-shallying.

When you have chosen your essay title and been given a submission date, make yourself a timetable, working backwards, from at least one day preceding the submission deadline (this will give you a little leeway for any last minute hiccup). Remember the stages you need to work through: collect your material, plan, draft, edit and finalise. Remember, also, to "factor in" other calls on your time - you might have other essays due in at the same time, a field trip to work around or a hospital appointment. Be realistic about how much time you have and start work on your essay as soon as you can.

If your essay is due in on a day when you will not be attending school/college/university, then submit early. Do not ask someone else to hand in your essay for you. It is your responsibility and nobody else will care as much about your work as you do.

Where?

The time at which you choose to write will also need to link into the location in which you like to work and this, in turn, will be governed by other factors. If you like to have a constant supply of coffee and snacks to keep your energy levels high while you work, then you need to work somewhere where you are able to cater to your own needs. You will feel distracted if you are hungry or thirsty. Likewise, if you are working anywhere other than at your home, then make sure you are comfortably dressed (preferably with an item of clothing that you can slip on or off as you feel you need it). You will not be able to concentrate fully if you are too hot or too cold.

If you really do feel you work better while listening to loud music or with a television on then you should choose somewhere to work where you will not be disturbing others and remember, even headphones do not mean that your music, or the bass notes at least, will not be distracting to others. A loud TV might not disturb you but, if your TV or music disturbs someone else then their complaining, or banging on the wall, will not aid your concentration. Be considerate.

If you know you do not work well alone, then try to find someone else who feels the same and, in a mutually convenient location, you can work together – as long as you really are both working and it is not an arrangement that leads to time-wasting or that suits one of you better than the other so only one of you is producing good work.

If you like to work without interruption, in peace and quiet, make sure this is understood by those around you. Turn off your phone and set time aside – then stick to it. Tell your friends and/or family that you will be working and do not want to be disturbed. When you have finished, you can catch up with friends or make phone calls with the satisfaction of knowing that you have produced some really good work.

You should always work where you are comfortable and well-supported physically. A decent chair and table/desk of the right height are ideal but, wherever you work, make yourself comfortable enough to avoid the pain which can be caused by long periods sitting in an awkward position (but not so comfortable that you risk falling asleep!). If you like to work outside, remember to use sun protection.

Wherever you choose to work, when you are ready to plan and draft your essay, make sure that you have all the tools you like to use to hand: several ball-point pens or pencils (with a sharpener) highlighters, erasers, post-it notes, stapler/paper clips etc., and a wide-lined, A4 pad. It is irritating to start working, full of enthusiasm, only to have to break off again to seek out another pen or a pencil sharpener.

If you are accustomed to drafting to computer successfully then there is no need to change the way you work. You must still keep a note of your references and your WP package "footnote" facility is probably the best way of achieving this. Your WP package should rearrange the footnotes if you rearrange your text. Use your "clipboard" facility to help you keep track of text you have "cut" until you have "pasted" it into the correct place. Remember to save your work regularly

However, if you prefer to hand-write your draft, then you will be able to work with your source materials to hand. A handwritten draft is easy to carry with you and work on whenever you get the opportunity (without the need for a laptop or access to a computer). It is easy to add margin notes to a handwritten draft and to note your references alongside your written text. A handwritten draft can be adjusted with less risk of losing anything (remember that the term "cut and paste" did not enter the language with the advent of the computer, it originally referred to the physical act of cutting out text and pasting it into a different position. If you cut a paragraph or section of your essay with scissors, it remains on your desk or table, in front of you, until you tape it into a different position).

With either method, though, it is essential that you check your references before submitting your essay. If you use *ibid* (meaning "in the same place" as the previous reference) or *op cit* (meaning "as previously mentioned") then you must ensure that these abbreviations are appropriate. If you rearrange text and the references to which these phrases refer no longer precede them, then the abbreviations are of no use. If you are not as familiar as you would like to be with computers, ask if your university or college has on-line tutorials for basic IT skills.

<u>CHOOSING WHEN AND WHERE</u> – <u>key points:</u>

- Do not waste your time.

- Make yourself a timetable and try to stick to it.

- Make sure you have everything you will need to use before you start working.

- Work at a time and in a place that suits you.

****

iv.   Organising your material and planning your essay

Having chosen your essay title, now is the time to make a brief essay plan and collect together the resources (books, photocopies, lecture notes, quotes from radio or TV etc) which you will need to use. As you focus on your essay, you will be able to be more selective about what will be useful to you. Some of those books initially borrowed from the library might now seem less relevant – these can be returned or put to one side. Keep your essay title written, in front of you, while you work. This will help you stay focused on your subject.

You will, almost certainly, have looked on the internet while doing your research and it would be ridiculous to ignore its value and potential as a tool to be used in essay writing but please exercise caution. Do not use the internet as your only source. Your tutors will be looking for evidence of the depth and breadth of your reading. If you are going to use something found on the internet, make sure it is accurate.

Some students spend a good deal of time reading, finding quotes and taking notes of reference material before starting to plan their essay. Others skim-read texts to start with then plan their essay – returning to read the texts more closely when they want to find quotes to support their arguments. You will find which way suits you best but, however you choose to work, when thinking about the quotes you are going to use, it helps to ask the following questions:

• Who said/wrote this?

- When?

- Why?

Be aware that the writer might have had her/his own agenda or the writing could be biased or malicious. The writer could have written for profit or to promote a certain viewpoint. It is always useful to bear these questions in mind but remember that, while an author whose work has been broadcast or published conventionally might be guilty of having had an ulterior motive for what has been said or written, she or he will, at least, have had to go through certain stages before her or his work has been presented to the public and the work will have been seen by other people (agents, broadcasting companies, producers etc) who might have exercised some editorial power. The internet can remove those stages so that extreme care is needed when relying on a downloaded source to support an argument.

Many students ask how many quotations they should use in an essay. It is impossible to say. There is no ideal number. You should write in a style that is natural to you and, when you make a point, back it up with evidence – and reference *every* piece of evidence you use. If you are really feeling anxious about the number of quotes to use then look at your essay questions and decide how many parts it contains (usually one or two questions). Decide how many points you want to cover for each part of the essay question. Each of these points will merit at least one paragraph and at least one quote. As you write, you might want to use more quotes to illustrate what you are saying but you should not use fewer quotes than the number of points you make.

Your plan

You will probably have heard other students say that, when writing an essay, you should "tell them what you're going to say; say it; then tell them what you've said". The fact that this advice has been repeated so often over the years would seem to indicate that there is an element of truth in it. Certainly, an essay has three main parts: the introduction, the main body and the conclusion. There should be a natural, logical progression from the title through to the conclusion and your reader's attention should be engaged and sustained by an objective, focused, interesting and informative piece of work.

The main body of your essay should account for about 75% of your work with the remaining 25% used, as required, in your introduction and conclusion. At this stage it is not necessary (perhaps not even advisable) to write too much. A few sentences to help you focus on the key words and decide exactly what you want your essay to say are all that you need in a plan.

Introduction

An introduction should be brief (no more than c10% of your total word allowance). It should engage the reader's attention immediately and it should:

- be concise (do not waffle)

- expand on the essay title, focusing on the key words (explain what it means to you)

- give an outline of what you intend to say in your essay

For some subjects it would be appropriate, in an introduction, to set the essay topic into context. Nothing happens in isolation. There will have been reasons for a new theory, policy or movement becoming popular or current at a certain time. A short paragraph giving some background to the essay topic might be useful.

The main body

Depending upon what you have been asked to do in the essay title (discuss…, compare and contrast…., criticise….) in the main body of your essay you should plan to give, for instance:

- an investigation and discussion of the main aspects of the question

- a review of the key debates in the topic area, referring to major theorists and outlining their theories

- a comparison of the main theories, focusing on the major similarities and differences, or an assessment of the most significant points referred to, or alluded to, in the essay question.

- your arguments and/or conclusion (supported by evidence)

Look at the essay titles at the end of this section with examples of the kind of preliminary questions which you might ask yourself to help you start thinking about a plan and the main points of an essay. You might not be able to address every question or point you think of initially but, underlining the key words in an essay title and then asking questions around the main points in this way, will help you to be focused in your research and to get you started on thinking about what you intend to cover with your writing. Remember to keep your essay title in front of you at all times.

Conclusion

Your conclusion should offer a very brief summary of the main points of your essay, and show how you have addressed the questions/points raised by the title. It should show how your research has added to the debate, or if it supports/disproves another researcher's findings.

Once you have an idea of your plan you should start a quick, short "brainstorming" exercise. Write quickly and spontaneously and write everything. Do not worry about spelling or grammar at this stage, the idea is to get your ideas written down as they come to you. You should not even be over-concerned about the order of your ideas – at this stage they will overlap and connect in different ways and it will be easy to re-organise them when you write your first draft.

If you have been making notes on a pad since deciding on your essay title, now is the time to collect them all together.

This brainstorming exercise should not take you too long. It should be quick and intense. Once finished, if you are intending to launch yourself straight into writing your first draft, you might find it helpful to give yourself a short break first.

<u>Now read the key points overleaf.</u>

ORGANISING AND PLANNING – key points:

- Make a plan by asking yourself questions which focus on the key words in your essay title.

- Collect useful resources – Do not use the internet as your only research source.

- "Brainstorm" your ideas.

- Take a break.

****

SAMPLE ESSAY TITLES WITH PRELIMINARY QUESTIONS

Essay title:	Preliminary questions:
"How were English ethnic identities constructed in the anti-slavery movement?"*	What do we mean by ethnic identity? What is specific about <u>English</u> ethnic identities? Look at slavery and pro-slavery lobby (participation in the slave trade, profit, what were their justifications? – with evidence). Look at anti-slavery movement (explain slavery/slave trade, duration, opposition, appeal of movement. Why at this time? – with evidence). How did this movement affect the construction of English ethnic identities? (with evidence) and has this identity persisted?
"Examine the Surrealist construction of woman and show why was she so central to their interests"	Who were the Surrealists? Why were they called that? When did they work? How did they construct "woman"? (give examples and some context – did this differ from how women were generally perceived in society at the time?). Why did they perceive "woman" in this way? (give evidence to support your reasoning). Why was she was so central to their interests? (give evidence)

"How could we distinguish between sound hopes and illusory hopes"*	Define hope. What are sound hopes? Who said so? What are illusory hopes? Who said so? What are the similarities? What factors should we use to distinguish between them? (with evidence)
"Explain how phonetics and phonology could be treated together rather than as distinct subjects"*	Define phonetics. Define phonology. What are the similarities? What are the differences? Give examples of how they have been treated as distinct subjects. Give reasons why they should be treated together (with evidence).
"What are the reasons for some regions of Britain being dominated by dispersed settlements and other regions by nucleated settlements"	What do we mean by dispersed settlements and nucleated settlements? (definitions + examples) What is distinctive about these settlement patterns? (Main characteristics) What are the main reasons why some regions are dominated by DS and some by NS? (be consistent. state whether looking at eco/social/political/geo factors (or all).

v.   Your first draft

This is the time to get all your ideas into order. Your plan will remind you of the sequence in which you want to make points in your essay, and your brainstorming exercise will have brought all your ideas to the forefront of your mind. You will have all the quotes you need (or might need) to hand, fully referenced. You are comfortable and have everything else you need to keep you going easily available. Before writing your essay there are two things to remember:

- Do NOT Plagiarise

- DO follow instructions

Plagiarism

The first, and the most important, fact to keep in mind is that this is your essay. You can write a good essay if you put in the effort. You must *never* try to pass off the work of somebody else as your own. This is cheating and it applies whether you copy a phrase or a whole essay. It is called plagiarism and it constitutes a serious academic offence. Furthermore, if you are caught trying to pass off somebody else's work as your own, then your essay will be given a "fail" grade.

A copied passage, written in a style that is different from your own, will be obvious to your reader. Also, your tutors will have spent several years *at least* studying the subject on which your essay is set. They will be familiar with all the current literature on the subject and with the history and theories which have given rise to contemporary thinking. They will also be aware of the source of most (if not all) of the quotes you are likely to find to support, or make a critique of, established work in your essay. You are almost certain to be detected if you try to cheat.

You will, of course, need to quote from source material in your essays – to support your ideas, to illustrate points you wish to make, to show different theorists' perspectives on your subject etc. Your quotes *MUST* be properly referenced whether they are taken from books, journals, newspapers, magazines, lecture notes or handouts. There will be more about referencing in Chapter 3 but, for now, it bears repeating that, every time you write down a quote that you are going to use, or think you might use, you should also write down the author's name, the date and place of publication, the title of the source, the publisher and page number(s).

Remember to remain aware that extra caution should be used to ensure the accuracy of material downloaded from the internet. It might be useful, it might not, but - if you do find a piece of relevant, accurate, usable material – it must still be referenced in exactly the same way (with full website address and date of download). You will be aware that there are websites which will sell you essays written by somebody else (most likely a recent graduate, being exploited by a go-between and under extreme pressure to turn out essays from home for people like you all day, every day, for the minimum wage) and it might seem like an easy option to purchase one of these essays and save yourself the effort of writing. Give the matter a little thought, though.

- If you have not bothered to research your subject enough to write a decent essay yourself, how will you know if the essay you buy is really appropriate and good enough to submit?

- Even if the essay is appropriate, how can you be sure that you will be the first, or only, person in your subject group to download and use it? (and, if you are not, then your tutors will most certainly recognise it).

- Your university or college will probably have access to sophisticated detection programmes designed to identify instances of plagiarism.

- Researching and writing a good essay can be a source of enormous satisfaction – copying someone else's work is never satisfying.

If you feel you need advice about resources, or if you think it would be useful to read someone else's essay on a similar subject, to see how it has been structured, then speak to your tutor. She or he will be able to point you in the right direction to get more support or help with your academic work.

Follow the instructions

Once the writing of your essay is underway, you will become engaged with your subject and gain an increased interest in the research you have done, and are doing. It is very easy to get sidetracked by a really riveting or innovative article, or passage in a book, and lose direction in your work. It bears repeating that you should refer constantly to the essay title and ensure that you follow the instructions given within it. The instructions given in the title will tell you exactly what your tutor expects you to do in your essay. The title will include words like:

- Compare and contrast (i.e. look for similarities and differences)

- Criticise/critically assess (i.e. analyse and evaluate)

- Define (i.e. state the precise meaning of a word or phrase)

- Describe (i.e. give a detailed account of)

- Discuss (i.e. investigate and look at both sides)

- Evaluate (i.e. examine and assess the worth of something)

- Explain (i.e. make clear and give the worth of something)

- Give the causes and effects of (i.e. describe something that has an effect (the cause) and also describe that effect)

- Outline and account for (i.e. give a general description of, or the main points of something and explain the reason(s) for its occurrence)

In general, you will be asked to do one of the following:

o look at both sides of an argument, comparing the similarities and differences
o address a point in detail - defining, explaining or clarifying by looking in depth at the different aspects
o summarise, outline or trace a theory or policy, referring to main points, rather than details

o criticise or disagree with a statement, giving your reasons and evidence

This is just a guide. You *must* follow the instruction(s) in the essay title. If you are unsure of the meaning of the title, or what is expected of you, ask your tutor to explain further.

Your essay is based on your own research and you might have made judgements about what you have read, or even drawn conclusions about the validity of an argument. You can give your own opinion or judgement in an essay as long as you are able to justify and support it with sound reasoning and evidence. Before you continue, check that what you have in your plan matches what is being asked of you in the essay title.

The first draft

When writing your first draft, continue to keep your essay title written out in front of you at all times and check regularly that you are not wandering from the subject. It is impossible to over-emphasise how easy it is to lose your focus when you are surrounded by the interesting works of other people. If you find something irresistible you can return to it but, right now, you are writing this essay and you must keep focused.

Now is the time to get your "brainstormed" notes into order so that they correspond with your initial plan. You should allocate them to "intro", "body" and "conclusion" but do not discard any yet. Try to include all your relevant ideas - if you put in everything you want to write at this stage, then your enthusiasm for your subject will be evident, even though you might have to edit your work heavily later.

Having separated their notes and quotes to correspond with the three sections of their essay, some students find it helpful to draft their conclusion first. Keeping a conclusion in mind, and the title in front of them, means that they are constantly reminded of the direction their essay should be taking.

Many students write their essay according to their plan but then finalise the wording of their introduction after having written the remainder of the essay. This gives them the chance to incorporate what they have actually said, or learned, while writing their essay into what they intended to say.

In the unlikely event that you feel you have had no choice but to write an essay on a topic for which you have little enthusiasm, try to make up for that with scrupulous research, careful writing and flawless presentation.

When you start to draft, do not use scruffy scraps of paper. Your work is worth more than that. Use a wide-lined, A4 pad. Write on one side of each sheet only and either write on alternate lines or leave extra space between paragraphs. This will make your work easier to read and, also, you will be able to add notes or references as you work or when you go back to edit your draft. While working, either keep your work on the pad or, if you remove the sheets as you fill them, make sure you keep everything together. Staple or clip the sheets in order (number the pages) and keep them safe in plastic pocket or ring binder. Remember, always, to keep reference information with the relevant quotes. That way, if you change the position of paragraphs or passages, you will not lose track of your quotes or of your references. Using your "brainstormed" notes and the answers to the preliminary questions you asked yourself around the key words of your essay title, you are now ready to write a properly structured, well-researched and informed essay.

While writing your essay you will probably experience a wide range of emotions, from despair at the volume of work involved and the length of time it takes, to elation when you find exactly the right quote to insert into a paragraph so that it sums up perfectly what you want to say. You might feel tired, frustrated and insecure at times but you *can* do it and, if you are focused in your research, approach your draft methodically and apply yourself diligently to your writing, then there is no reason why you should not achieve a good mark.

When things start to get difficult, or even a bit boring, there is always a tendency to read through what has already been written. However, you should resist this temptation. It is better to take a five-minute break at times like these than to start to go back over what you have written and edit or change things before you have finished. You need to go forward and you cannot do that while constantly reading and re-reading only part of your essay. Finish your draft, give yourself a decent break and then do a complete review of what you have written.

<u>Now read the key points overleaf.</u>

THE FIRST DRAFT – key points:

- Do not plagiarise.

- Refer frequently to the essay title and follow the instructions in it.

- Keep your notes organised.

- Make sure you keep each quote and the relevant reference material together.

****

Chapter 2

The Review

---

i.   Reviewing Your Draft

Try to give yourself a break between finishing and reviewing your first draft. If you approach your work afresh, you will probably be surprised at how quickly and easily you can identify ways of improving what you have written, just by rearranging a couple of paragraphs or rephrasing a sentence.

If, when you read through your essay, you feel that there is scope for improvement but you find it difficult to identify the changes that need to be made, think about the language you have used and the way you have chosen to give the information contained in your essay to your reader.

If you are working on a computer, then you need to be very careful not to make errors when you are editing. Save your work frequently. It is a good idea to "copy" your work to a new folder, giving it a slightly different name (e.g. "October Essay, no: 2"). Make your alterations to the document in the new folder. If you should then have an editing disaster or become confused at some stage, you can return to your original draft, having lost nothing, and start again, with care.

If your draft is hand-written, do not rewrite the whole essay at this stage. Read through your work and mark alterations with a highlighter or with a pen of a different colour. Write any additions in the margin or on the back of the previous page but make sure that you mark very clearly where the new text is stored and where it is to be inserted.

Language

If you are not used to writing academic essays but have read academic journals, you might have felt intimidated by the language used. If you feel that the language you customarily use to express yourself is too informal for an essay, it is not difficult to get into the habit of writing in a more formal way - without making your writing sound pretentious. You should not use abbreviations in your writing: (use "do not", instead of "don't", use "is not" instead of "isn't", etc.); never use slang and avoid the use of colloquialisms or jargon.

You will possibly, but not necessarily, write the opening paragraph of the introduction to your essay in the first person singular (using "I"). After expanding on the essay title, you might go on to say, for example:

o   "In this essay I will look at the reasons why….."

o   "In this essay I will attempt to show that…."

o   "In this essay I will argue that…."

After the introduction, your essay will be improved by the use of the "passive voice". For instance:

- Instead of saying "I am now going to look at...", you could say "Turning now to ..."

- Instead of saying "I will show that..." you could say "It can be seen that..."

- Instead of saying "I think ..." you could say "Evidence suggests that ..."

- Instead of saying "I have looked at different theories and I think...." you could say "Having examined various theorists' views, it can be seen that..."

It is not difficult to write in this way and it has the added advantage, for you, of making it easier to retain the focus of the sentence. When we start a sentence with "I", we often become too subjective; when we use the passive voice it keeps our writing objective and objectivity is essential when writing academic essays.

While discussing the language you will use in your essays, do remember that you must not use any language which may be construed as racist, sexist or homophobic, or which discriminates against people in any way because of their ethnicity, race, gender, sexuality or religion.

Some old sources will use masculine words exclusively (He, him, his etc). Such language today would be considered sexist and, in your own writing you should use, for instance, "S/he", "her or himself", "her or his" etc. However, if you are directly quoting exclusively masculine pronouns (he, him) or adjectives (his), include the word *(sic)* after them to indicate that these words appear in the original source.

For example:

> "Hence, the cost of production of a workman *(sic)* is restricted, almost entirely, to the means of subsistence that he *(sic)* requires for his *(sic)* maintenance, and for the propagation of his *(sic)* race"[1]

Similarly, *(sic)* can be used if there was an error in the original text or quote. The extract should be copied exactly but *(sic)* - meaning "so" - shows that you are aware of the inaccuracy.

Communicating fluently

When we have a face-to-face conversation with someone else, we not only listen to the words the person is saying, we also pick up clues to the meaning of those words from their facial expression, body language, hand gestures and tone of voice. In writing, however, we must be especially careful of the construction of our work – the "signposting", punctuation, spelling and grammar – in order to ensure that the piece we have written actually means what we want it to mean, and that the sense of our work is not lost because the reader is having

---

[1] Marx, K. Engels, F. (1848) "The Communist Manifesto". Tr: Moore, S. (1888).

difficulty understanding our grammar, deciphering our spelling or being led astray by our punctuation.

When you write your essay, you will divide it into its three main components (intro, body, conclusion) but these, in turn, will be divided into paragraphs, which in their turn will consist of sentences.

Sentences

A sentence usually has a subject (a noun, or noun phrase which denotes the "doer" or "receiver" of an action) or the thing that the sentence is describing, and a predicate (which will contain a finite verb or a verb phrase).

However, the important point to remember about a "sentence" is that it must always be a complete unit, which can be understood alone. A sentence can consist of a single word, several words or several phrases, separated by commas or other punctuation.

For instance, the word "Stop!" can be a sentence but the word "tablet" cannot. "Stop" is a verb and, implicit in its use, is the assumption that there is a subject (the person who is being told to "stop").

"The boy walked down the road" is also a sentence. It makes sense alone (it has a subject: the boy, and it tells us what the boy did, in the verb phrase "walked down the road").

However, this longer group of words, taken from an undergraduate essay (and which can, similarly, be understood alone), also constitutes a sentence:

> "The concept of 'collective consciousness', then, plays a major role in Durkheim's theory of society and, central to his thoughts on social solidarity was a concern with the characteristics of modern society (eg secularism and individualism) which he believed could lead to a fragmentation of society."

You are unlikely to use any single-word sentences in your essay and, if you use long sentences, you must be careful not to make them so long as to confuse your reader. A sentence should make a point and make sense. Your essay will be easier, and more interesting to read, if you try to use sentences of varying lengths. (When you have written your essay it is always a good idea to get somebody else to read it, or to read it aloud to yourself, so that you can hear if it "flows". You will be able to tell if your work sounds awkward (with sentences that are too short) or confusing (with sentences that are too long). Reading aloud is also a useful exercise while you are in the process of writing, too. If you have doubts about the construction, or the length, of a sentence, saying it aloud will help you to decide if it makes sense and whether or not it needs to be changed.)

Paragraphs

A paragraph is a distinct section of your essay, which will usually consist of several sentences which link ideas. Each paragraph should deal with a major aspect of your essay so a new paragraph should occur naturally, where you change from one idea or theme to another. The main point of the paragraph should be made in the first sentence.

Paragraphs are separated by inserting an extra line-space between them. Your paragraphs should not be too long. If you are clear about what you want to say, and your writing is concise, then your paragraph breaks will occur without your having to worry too much about their position. If a paragraph does seem to be dragging on and becoming too long, reread it and rephrase it if necessary. You might find that it then falls quite easily into two separate sections – in which case, you could divide it into two paragraphs. If that does not happen, and you really cannot see a way of reducing its length, then mark it with a highlighter or coloured pen, and return to it later when you might be able to deal with it more easily.

Remember, it is daunting for a reader to face a page of solid typescript, or handwriting, with no paragraph breaks.

Signposting

By the time you come to collate your ideas and write your first draft, you will be very familiar with the ideas in your essay. When you read it through, you will know where the initial ideas are going to lead and there will be obvious (to you) links between points you are making. Your tutor will not have the advantage of this knowledge. From time to time you should give an indication that you are moving on to a different point, so that your reader can understand where your ideas are leading, or even insert a reminder of the stage you have reached with your argument, and where your thoughts go next. (Not only will this help your reader, it will also help you to stay "on track").

This is called "signposting" and is placed at the beginning of a paragraph where it us helpful to use words or phrases like:

- Moving on to ….

- Turning now to ……

- However …..

- On the other hand …….

- Similarly ….

- In the light of the above, it can be seen that …..

- Evidence suggests, though, that ….

Sometimes it is useful to recap on the previous paragraph, too:

- Having looked at ……., it is useful to examine …….

- It has been established that ……. but it can also be seen that…….

- It can be seen, then, that XX ……. On the other hand, however, YY would appear to indicate that……

- Briefly, then, we have seen that ….. and can now move on to look at …..

- Having dealt with ….. we can now look at …..

When you have reviewed your draft, ensured that you have included all the points you want to make and made any changes you think are necessary, you should be able to answer "yes" to the following questions:

1. Has everything been copied correctly from notes or other resources?

2. Does the essay make sense?

3. Is it well organised, clear and interesting?

4. Does the essay "flow" smoothly from the title to the conclusion, with adequate signposting?

5. Is every sentence an important part of the whole essay? (if not, think about re-writing that sentence or leaving it out completely).

6. Do all the quotes and the references match up?

7. Does the introduction capture the attention?

8. Does the conclusion offer a concise summing-up of all the points made?

You should, at this stage, do a "word count". You still have some work to do on your essay so your word count will change a little but you should, by now, be reasonably close to your tutor's requirements.

You might have been given a range to aim for (e.g. 2,000 – 2,500 words) or a number of pages (e.g. 8-10 pages in double-line spacing) but, if you have been given a single figure (e.g. 3,000 words) then it is likely that an essay within ± 10% of that figure will be acceptable. If your essay is considerably longer than permitted, do not worry - some judicious editing will address the problem. It is always irritating to have to remove from an essay a passage over which you have laboured but, sometimes, it has to be done. Remember that your research will not have been wasted. You will, almost certainly, be able to use the discarded information in a future essay, an exam or a seminar discussion.

If your essay is considerably shorter than it should be, then you probably have some more research and writing to do. Get started now. Look at what you have written. How much do you need to add? Whatever you add must be relevant; do not just go back into your essay and waffle but try to identify a genuine addition which will improve the work. Is there a point you have avoided making? Could you write about a theory which conflicts with one you have already mentioned? Could you add a second theorist's views in support of one you have written about? Is there a point in your essay which really needs some clarification?

You might need a short break to clear your mind so that, when you look again at your essay, it is easier to see a gap which can be filled. If you still cannot see where you can add some words, and you have time, leave your essay overnight and try not to get too anxious about it. Hopefully that will give you the space you need to relax and allow a solution to come, which it inevitably will.

<u>Now read the key points overleaf.</u>

REVIEWING YOUR DRAFT – key points:

- Read through your work and identify possible improvements.

- Go through the checklist of eight questions and make sure that you can answer "Yes" to all of them.

- Do a word-count and take action if necessary.

****

ii.   Spelling and using the right word

When you have reviewed your draft and are happy with what you have written, and how you have written it, take time to check your spelling, grammar and punctuation. If you already know that your work follows a logical course from the title through to the conclusion then some attention to detail will ensure that your essay is fluent and easy to understand.

The English language has evolved over the past two thousand years and has been influenced by many other languages in that time. It has not stopped changing and it will not stop in the future. Without this constant renewal we would still be addressing each other as "thee" and the word "text" would still be just a noun, rather than a verb as well. However, constant change does not mean that we can be careless about written work. We are still always bound by current conventions.

Reports from recruitment consultants suggest that about half of all CVs submitted to them contain errors in spelling or grammar – and these errors can make the difference between being offered a job or being unemployed. It is interesting that the worst offenders are graduates, who are twice as likely to make errors on their CVs than those who did not go to university. Getting into the habit of checking your work carefully will quickly increase your confidence in your written work and your ability to avoid the pitfalls which trap others.

To a linguistics expert, the word "grammar" means the scientific study of a language including the regularity of

61

structure, the meaning and arrangement of words, pronunciation and the history of words. However, colloquially, when we talk about "grammar" we usually mean using the right words, in the right order, in a well constructed and punctuated sentence so that the sentence can be read and understood by another person.

Using the right word is often a case of ensuring that we spell a word correctly and do not use a similar-sounding word which has a different spelling and meaning. A spell-check on a word processing package can help enormously by pointing up inconsistencies in grammar and spelling errors in your written work. However, it is seldom a good idea to rely on your computer alone.

Look at this sentence:

> *The boy wanted one but did not know if there were two or three so he went to Wales to find out.*

Now look at this sentence:

> *The buoy wanted won butt did knot no if their were to oar three sew he went too whales two find out.*

There are twenty-two words in each sentence, but there are *fourteen* errors in the second sentence – and not one shows up on a spell check!

This is an extreme example of how a spell-check can "miss" words which sound the same but have more than one spelling, but it does illustrate that there is still a place for the dictionary when we are unsure of how to spell a word in a particular context.

Some words, which sound the same but have different meanings and spellings, are frequently confused. It is interesting that the words advice (a noun) and advise (a verb) are never confused, nor are device and devise, because they have different pronunciations, but look at the other words here:

Advice -   a noun: *"She gave him advice"*

Advise -   a verb: *"He tried to advise her"*

Device -   a noun: *"I will use a different device this time"*

Devise -   a verb: *"Can you devise a new method for me?"*

Licence -   a noun: *"I do not have a driving licence"*

License -   a verb: *"Will you license me to sell alcohol?"*

Practice -   a noun: *"They went to football practice"*

Practise -   a verb: *"They had to practise hard for the match"*

"Advice" and "advise" are easily distinguishable in speech, as are "device" and "devise", but note that, when writing, the words licence/license and practice/practise follow the same pattern even though they sound the same. The noun version ends in *"~ice"* and the verb version ends in *"~ise"*. Generally, if you are unsure which version of the word to use, substitute "advice" or "advise" and read the sentence to yourself. It might not make much sense but it should help you to establish if you want the noun version or your word or the verb version.

Other words of which you should be aware are listed here with very brief definitions or reminders of how we generally use them. If you are still unsure about these words and their meanings, you should look them up in a dictionary.

Accept	To receive or believe something.
Except	When we exclude something.
Accede	To agree to someone's request, or to take up a position (e.g. *accede* to the throne).
Exceed	To go over or beyond (e.g. an amount or time).
Access	(noun) Ability to enter. Now also used as a verb, e.g. to *access* something on a computer.
Excess	Surplus.
Adaptor	A thing which adapts something else.

Adapter	A person who adapts something (e.g. a play for the cinema).
Adverse	Unfavourable.
Averse	Unwilling, not very keen.
Affect	To have an impact or influence on something.
Effect	A consequence (the impact caused by something else).
Allusion	A reference to something else.
Illusion	A trick or a false impression.
Bought	Past participle of the verb *to buy*: "I bought these shoes at the shop yesterday".
Brought	Past participle of the verb *to bring*: "He brought his CD over and lent it to me". She had been well brought up.
Complement	To go with something to complete or balance it.
Compliment	(verb) To say something nice about someone else. (Or (noun) the nice thing we say).
Council	Group of people meeting as an official body.
Counsel	To give advice.

Currant	Dried berry.
Current	Up to date <u>OR</u> flow of electricity/water.
Decade	Ten years.
Decayed	Decomposed.
Dependant	(noun) A person who needs or gets help or support.
Dependent	(adjective) This describes the person: "He is dependent upon his brother for help".
Descendant	(noun) A person who has descended down a line (family, royal).
Descendent	This adjective (which is now not often used) describes something that has descended.
Discreet	Diplomatic, tactful.
Discrete	Separate or distinct.
Elicit	To draw out (e.g. the truth about a matter).
Illicit	Unlawful.
Eminent	Distinguished
Imminent	About to happen

Ensure	To guarantee, or make sure something happens.
Insure	To take out insurance cover against loss or damage.
Flaunt	To show off.
Flout	To disobey or ignore rules or conventions.
Formally	describes doing something in an official way.
Formerly	Previously
Ingenious	Clever or inventive.
Ingenuous	Trusting, honest.
Loath	(adjective) Unwilling or reluctant.
Loathe	(verb) To despise.
Precede	To go before.
Proceed	To carry on or continue.
Paw	Animal's foot.
Poor	Deprived, lacking money and/or privilege.
Pore	(noun) Small hole in skin or membrane. (verb) To read closely – "pore" as a verb is used with "over" e.g. "They pored over the map".

Pour	To tip liquid out of a jug or other vessel.
Prescribe	To recommend.
Proscribe	To forbid.
Principal	(adjective) Main or most important, e.g. "My principal career is that of doctor".
	(noun) The head of a college is The Principal.
Principle	Code or standard, e.g. "She stuck to her principles".
	"In principle…" can also mean "In theory
Quash	To invalidate.
Squash	To crush or flatten.
Stationary	(adjective) Not moving.
Stationery	(noun) Items on which, or with which, we write. (An easy way to remember these two words is that station*e*ry includes *e*nvelopes).
Their	Belonging to them.
There	Denotes a place: "I'm going over there" or "There it is". (An easy way to remember this spelling is that it is *here* with a *"t"* added.

They're	An abbreviation of "They are".
To	<u>Always</u> use this version unless the context indicates use of the following:
Too	Means "also" (Can I go, too?) or "excessively" (e.g. too hot, too cold).
Two	A number.
Urban	Built-up (when referring to town or city area).
Urbane	Elegant, debonair.
Weather	Climate.
Whether	A word that indicates a choice: "I don't know whether or not to go"; "They couldn't decide whether to eat there, or here".
Whose	Indicates possession, e.g. "Do you know whose purse this is?" or "Whose name is on the document?"
Who's	Abbreviated form of "Who is", eg "Who's coming?", "Who's at the door?" or "She's the one who's going to do it".

Finally, the word that is so easy to remember if you have been taught how to recognise the correct spelling:

We <u>sep*a*rate</u> something into p*a*rts. (Never, ever *seperate*!)

REMEMBER - If you are not sure of a spelling – look it up in a dictionary!

Plurals

Most speakers of English will know that we make a singular word plural by adding *"s"*, e.g. book/books, chair/chairs etc. This rule also applies when a word ends in *"~ey"*, e.g. trolley/trolleys, monkey/monkeys, key/keys (the same rule used to apply to money/moneys but *"moneys"* is now seldom seen, except in legal documents, and the spelling *"monies"* has been accepted). If a word ends in *"~y"*, then we take away the *"y"* and add *"ies"*, e.g. hobby/hobbies, bully/bullies.

However, words ending in *"~is"*, which are Greek in origin, are made plural by changing the ending to *"~es"*

For example, when pluralised:

- One crisis   becomes   Two crises

- One diagnosis   becomes   Several diagnoses

- One thesis   becomes   Many theses

- One oasis   becomes   Some oases

Words ending in *"~on"*, (also Greek in origin) are made plural by changing the *"~on"* to *"~a"*.

70

For example, in the plural:

- Criterion   becomes   Criteria

- Phenomenon   becomes   Phenomena

Some plural formations are now considered unwieldy and are no longer used. For instance, words ending in *"~us"*, which have a Latin root, traditionally change to *"i"* to make the plural. *Terminus*, for example, became *Termini* in the plural. However, the plural *"Terminuses"* is now considered acceptable.

Similarly, words ending in *"~um"*, also with a Latin root, like *Forum*, would traditionally have become *Fora i*n the plural. However, the modern plural, *Forums* is more widely used and accepted today.

Miscellaneous

English language has many peculiarities which often confuse students. For example:

Comprise/comprising – do not need to be followed by *"of"* because they mean *consist of* and *consisting of.* For example: "This is a group comprising the fast runners".

Fewer/less than – if something can be counted, then we use the expression "fewer than" to denote a smaller quantity of that thing. If it cannot be counted, then we say "less than". For example: "There are fewer than a hundred books there" or

"There were fewer than ten people in the room"; but "There is less sugar in that bowl" or "There has been less snow this year".

<u>Myriad</u> – originally meant "ten thousand", is now used to mean *a vast number*. It does not need to be accompanied by either "a" or "of". It is used as "Myriad stars shone in the sky".

<u>Perfect/Unique</u> – are absolute adjectives. Usually there are degrees of description (we call them positive, comparative and superlative), for instance: big, bigger, biggest; good, better, best; new, newer, newest etc, but unique means "the only one of its kind" and perfect means "flawless". If something is unique, then nothing can be *more* unique. Similarly, if something is perfect, nothing can be *more* perfect.

<u>Now read the key points overleaf.</u>

SPELLING AND USING THE RIGHT WORD – key points:

- Check that you have used the right word in the right context.

- If you are not sure of a spelling – look it up in a dictionary.

- Do not rely on a computer spell-check.

****

iii.   **Punctuation**

Punctuation is not governed by hard and fast rules and so changes occur often, according to fashion. It is probably best not to get too bogged down by trying to use punctuation marks that are unnecessary. The ones to remember are:

Capital (upper-case) letters:

Many years ago, when pages of print were set by hand, each compositor had two divided, cover-less cases beside him (compositing was invariably a man's job) holding individual letters.

The case containing letters that were used constantly was mounted beside the compositor and easily reachable. The case containing the less-used letters was placed above the first case because it did not need to be so easily accessible. This case contained the capital letters (the "upper case" letters) while the case beneath it contained the more frequently used "lower case" letters.

We still use the expressions "upper case" and "lower case" to identify letters but fashions in the use of capital letters have changed frequently and, in very recent years, their use has declined quite dramatically.

In an attempt to attract attention, the titles of books, films or plays are now sometimes written without a capital letter, as are trade names, and these should always be copied as they appear. You should still always use a capital letter at the beginning of :

- a sentence

- the name of a person

- the name of a country, language or religion

If you are using a title with a person's name, then the title has an initial capital, too. For example, we would write Councillor Brown, or Doctor Jones but, if we were just writing about a doctor, or a councillor, then a lower case initial is correct.

Full stops:

A full stop marks the end of a sentence. Every sentence should end with a full stop unless it ends with a question mark or an exclamation mark (both of which incorporate a full stop). A question mark indicates the end of a direct question, e.g. "Are they going into town tonight?"; but an indirect question, e.g. "He asked if she was going into town tonight" does not need a question mark.

This is sometimes difficult to remember because of the increasing use, in recent years, of an upward inflection at the end of a sentence. This habit can make any sentence, or even a short phrase, sound like a question. A full stop comes immediately after the last letter of the final word in a sentence and, when typing, is followed by two spaces.

<u>Commas</u>:

- A comma marks a short pause within a sentence, e.g. "He asked her if she was going into town tonight, but she said she was going home instead".

- A comma is also used to separate a sub-clause when it precedes a main clause, e.g. "Having looked at the evidence, she decided that the verdict was correct".

- Commas can separate adjectives: "The person was a mean, nasty, unreliable, work shy rascal" or nouns: "They had ornaments, photographs, books and memorabilia on every flat surface in their house".

- A comma can be used after an adjective if it begins a sentence, e.g. "However, it is clear that this was not the case" or "Nevertheless, it soon became apparent that the experiment was flawed". When such adjectives appear *within* a sentence, commas can surround them, e.g. "It is clear, however, that this is not the case".

It is quite easy to work out whether or not you have put commas, and full stops, in the right places in your essay by reading your work through and pausing for a count of two for a comma and for a count of three for a full stop. If your sentence sounds right, then your punctuation is in the correct place. If you use too many commas, or if you have a full stop in the wrong place, your sentence will be difficult to understand. If this happens, try to rewrite the piece – perhaps dividing it into two separate sentences, or making a *précis* so that it is more concise and fewer words are used. There is no space between a comma and the preceding word.

Colons (:) and semicolons (;):

The colon is no longer frequently used. When it is used, it is generally to introduce a list or a quote, e.g.:

- The inventory included: a bronze statue, a gold watch and an antique writing desk.
- The minister said: "Thank you for your support".

A semicolon is used to indicate a longer pause than a comma, but a shorter pause than a full stop. When a semicolon joins two phrases of similar importance within a sentence, no "linking word" is necessary, e.g.:

- "Vote for me; I will work hard for you."
- "Put that down; it's dangerous."

There is never a space between a colon or a semi-colon and the preceding word.

The apostrophe:

An apostrophe is used either:
- to indicate possession

or

- to show that a letter, or letters, have been left out of a word.

When indicating possession, the apostrophe comes before the "s" if the owner is a single person or thing, and after the "s" if there is more than one owner.

So:

- The boy's books –   means the books belonging to one boy

- The boys' books –   means the books belonging to some boys

- The girl's pens   –   means the pens belonging to one girl

- The girls' pens   –   means the pens belonging to some girls

- The dog's kennel–   means the kennel belonging to one dog

- The dogs' kennel –   means the kennel belonging to some dogs

A very traditional way of remembering where to place an apostrophe is to break down the phrase or sentence and to think about its meaning. For instance:

The girl, her pens

The boy, his books

The dog, its kennels

In each case, when an apostrophe is used, it is placed <u>before</u> the "*s*" (becoming "The girl's pen", "The boy's book", "The dog's kennel" etc). However, if we want to say:

The girls, their pens

The boys, their books

The dogs, their kennels

then the apostrophe is placed <u>after</u> the final "*s*" (becoming "the girls' pens", "the boys' books", "The dogs' kennels" etc).

Plurals that are made without adding "~*s*" or "~*es*", for instance: children, women, men, take an apostrophe, followed by an "*s*" to indicate possession:

• The children's toys

• The women's cars

• The men's books

NEVER use an apostrophe with a possessive pronoun: his, hers, theirs, its, ours.

The apostrophe is also used where letters have been taken out of words to make them informal (not appropriate in essay writing).

You are	becomes	You're
You are not	becomes	You're not
You will	becomes	You'll
You will not	becomes	You won't
I will	becomes	I'll
I will not	becomes	I won't
I am	becomes	I'm
I am not	becomes	I'm not
It is not	becomes	It isn't
I could have	becomes	I could've
I should have	becomes	I should've (not "I should *of..*")
It **is**	becomes	It's

(but there is never an apostrophe in the possessive pronoun *"its"* - as in the cat licked *its* bowl clean" or "My dog enjoyed *its* bone")

<u>Now read the key points overleaf.</u>

PUNCTUATION – key points:

- Check that your punctuation is appropriate
- Check for misplaced apostrophes

- Check that you have not used any abbreviations

****

iv.   Readability

When you write your essay, you should have a reader in mind who is intelligent and interested, and who wants to learn more about the subject of your essay. Do not "write down" or patronise any potential reader but do not try to write in a pretentious, unnatural way either.

You will probably have heard of "readability scores" and you can find out how to use scoring facilities by using the on-screen "Help" menu on your WP package.

Readability scores rate a passage (or a whole essay) for ease of reading by using a formula which calculates the average sentence length and average number of syllables per word. These calculations can give a score out of 100 where the higher the score, the easier it is to understand the content. You will be familiar with the difference in writing between tabloid newspapers and broadsheets and it is likely that, if an article was selected at random from each kind of newspaper, the article in the tabloid would have a higher readability score than an article in the broadsheet newspaper.

As an example, this passage from an undergraduate essay has a score of 24.3:

> "We continue in our efforts to quantify the effect of
>
> education by "testing" and we underline the value placed
>
> by society on credentials by so arranging education that

the majority of school-leavers possess a "certificate" to carry with them in their search for work (an increasingly fruitless task – with or without credentials). We still place an inordinate value on certain kinds of knowledge (that acquired in "school", to the exclusion of that acquired elsewhere) for its effect on others."

While the sentence below, making the same points, has a score of 98:

"We still test kids at school. They leave with bits of paper. They use these to find a job. That's tough these days. We say what they learn at school is good."

It is not difficult to see why these two passages have vastly differing readability scores and you might think it would help to score your own work in this way in order to give you some idea of the level your writing achieves.

Remember to bear in mind, though, that a readability score will give you an *average* mark for the whole of the piece of work you are checking and do be aware that it is still up to you to ensure that your essay makes sense, and to decide what kind of score you would like to achieve.

The following sentence has a readability score of 40.7 (approximately mid-way between the two earlier examples) but, clearly, it is nonsense:

> "It has been proved by generations of eminent scientists that the sun revolves around the earth at exactly thirteen miles an hour. Meanwhile, the earth rotates on its own axis at a speed of approximately seventeen trillion metres per second. While some prominent sceptics are currently disputing these figures, it is unlikely that their work will lead to any adjustment to the accepted data and their efforts will, eventually, be seen as misguided."

Remember: readability scores can be useful but that they to not claim to assess content.

<u>Now read the key points overleaf.</u>

<u>READABILITY – key points:</u>

- Keep your reader in mind at all times as you review your essay
- Remember that "Readability" gives no indication of content quality
- If you are going to score your whole essay for "readability", remember that the score will be an *average* for the whole piece

****

Chapter 3

The Crucial Details

---

i. The final check

Now that you have reviewed your draft, and made any necessary corrections or alterations, it is a good idea to make one final check to ensure that your essay makes sense and flows coherently. The easiest way to do this is either to read the essay aloud to yourself, ensuring that your punctuation and signposting indicate where there should be a pause or a change of direction or, even better, to get somebody else to read it for you.

If you have a partner, parent or friend who is willing to read your draft and comment truthfully and constructively on it, then enlist their help. Someone who is not familiar with the subject matter of your essay will be able to judge easily whether or not it is fluent. If your essay is clumsy, or if you have repeated information, somebody who is reading your work for the first time will see this much more easily than you will.

If you have removed a section of your essay, or a paragraph, you must be careful that what remains still makes sense. Sometimes we read the remainder of a piece of work we have edited and retain in our minds the section we have removed.

This can leave us with the mistaken impression that no meaning has been lost. Someone approaching your work for the first time, to read it for you, will spot something like this immediately.

Some students make up their own novel ways of checking their essays – for instance, reading all the sentences in reverse order. This, apparently, makes a misplaced phrase or a repetition immediately obvious. You will find which way suits you best but, for now, do ensure that you make this final check, whichever method you use, before carefully copying everything into your final version for submission.

<u>Now read the key points overleaf.</u>

THE FINAL CHECK – key points:

- Read your essay aloud or ask someone else to read it for you.

- Look for clumsy sentences, repetition and editing errors.

- If your draft is handwritten, take care to copy it up accurately.

****

ii.   Quotations

Students often feel anxious about referencing and paraphrasing but, as long as you are careful, never try to pass someone else's work of as your own and give your reader full referencing information, then you will soon get used to the conventions.

If you use a piece of information which is in the public domain and taken for granted, then you would not need to ascribe it to another writer but, when you refer to another writer's work to make a point (whether the work is published or unpublished and whether you quote directly from the piece or not) you should always give your tutors the information they will require to trace the passage.

Think of your reader finding a piece of information in your essay and wondering "Where did that come from?" Your reference should provide the answer. If you make a statement in an essay without a quote and reference to support it, it is very likely that, when your essay has been marked, you will find the question "Who said this?" in the margin.

Some quotes will be short, a few words, while others will be longer, perhaps several lines. However, you should avoid using too many very long quotes because that could give your reader the impression either that you have not really understood the point you are making, or that you have not bothered to work out what is being said for yourself. If you use a quote which contains words which you feel are unnecessary within the context of your essay, then you can leave them out, but you should mark their omission with suspension points (a series of dots). For instance, the paragraph:

> "The vendor is bound to take reasonable care of the property and should not let the property fall into disrepair or other damages to be caused during the period between exchange and completion."[1]

could be shortened, for your essay, to:

> "The vendor is bound to take reasonable care of the property ... between exchange and completion"[2].

If you wanted to use a quote as *part* of a sentence and needed to adjust a word to "fit" with what you wanted to say, then you should use square brackets to mark the change. For instance:

> The vendor still occupies the property and "is bound to take reasonable care of ... [it] ... between exchange and completion"[3].

Inclusion of quotes:

If a quote you use is short, up to two lines, then it can be presented, in quotation marks, within the text of your essay. If it is longer, then it should be indented and in single-line

---

[1] James, F. (2006) The Process of Conveyancing. (Edn. 2) Brighton: Straightforward Publishing. (p.57)
[2] *ibid*
[3] *ibid*

spacing, with an extra line space above and below it so that it stands out clearly from the rest of the essay. It is not essential to use quotation marks for such a large quote but some departments stipulate that you must use them for all quotes, whatever the length.

You must always copy quoted material accurately. Do not use underlining or italic font to emphasise any part that is not emphasised in the original. If you want to emphasise a word, or part of the quote *yourself*, you should make it clear that you have done so by adding the words "my emphasis", in brackets, at the end of the quote.

<u>Now read the key points overleaf.</u>

<u>QUOTATIONS – key points:</u>

- Support every point you make with a quotation.

- Give full reference information for *every* quote you use.

- Always copy quotations accurately and, if you omit any part of a quote, indicate that you have done so.

- Do not use too many very long quotes.

iii.　Referencing

The information required for a reference is:

- Name of author, in capital letters, with initial(s)

- Date of publication (in brackets)

- Title of publication - underlined, **bold** or in *italics*. (If your department does not specify a style, then you may choose, but be consistent throughout your references)

- Edition number (if not the first edition)

- Place of publication and name of publishers

- Pages referred to

For example, for a quote from page 10 of the third edition of a fictitious book called "Digging holes with ease", by Monty Mole, published in 2006 in New York by Tunnel Publishing Inc the reference would be:

MOLE, M. (2006) **Digging holes with ease**. (3rd edn). New York: Tunnel Publishing, Inc. (p.10)

If the book had been written by Brian Badger and Monty Mole, then the reference would be:

BADGER, B. and MOLE, M. (2006) Digging holes with ease. (3rd edn). New York: Tunnel Publishing, Inc. (p.10).

However if there were, for example, five authors listed, you could write:

BADGER, B. MOLE, M. *et al* (2006) *Digging holes with ease.* (3rd edn). New York: Tunnel Publishing, Inc. (p.10).

(*et al* means "and others").

The names of authors should always be given in the order in which they appear in the publication.

If you are quoting from an edited anthology then you need to include information about the original source and information about the anthology.

For instance, if the quote you are using comes from another fictitious work, an original publication called "Climbing Mountains" (the primary source), written by Andrew Able in 1920, but you are quoting from a secondary source then you must reference both. If, instead of reading the original publication, you took your quote from the first edition of an anthology called "Exciting Stories" edited by Bernice Brown and Charles Cook, published in 2005 in London by Sticky Publishing plc, then your reference would be:

ABLE, A. (1920) 'Climbing Mountains'. In: BROWN, B. and COOKE C., (eds) (2005) Exciting Stories. London: Sticky Publishing plc. (pp 6-7)

(Note that, if your quote starts on one page of a book and finishes on the next, then the use of the letters "pp" with both page numbers, is appropriate).

Other sources

When referring to a newspaper/magazine/periodical article – add the title of the publication after the title of the article (which has been emphasised by underlining, emboldening or italicising as above). Also add the volume or issue number. (The date of publication is especially important when referring to frequently published media).

For broadcast material, a series title (if appropriate) should be added after the programme title. The names of the director and writer (if available) should be added with the date of transmission and the medium (with channel).

The referencing of material accessed in electronic format is comparatively new but, as with all other referencing, you must be consistent and give your reader all the information required to trace your quote. In addition, you must give the full URL ("Uniform Resource Locator", previously "Universal Resource Locator") and the date on which you downloaded the material.

If you are quoting from an unpublished work, you should add the degree for which it was submitted, the university and the year of submission, for example:

COOPER, D. J. (1989) 'Studies on high gravity brewing and its negative effect on beer foam stability'. PhD Thesis (unpublished). Heriot Watt University, Edinburgh.

or

YOUNG, M. (1994) *A Study Into the Reasons Why Ex-Prisoners Reoffend*. BA Dissertation (unpublished). University of Essex.

(Note that some universities stipulate that unpublished work should be enclosed within single quotation marks).

Presenting your references
There are several different ways to present your references – references in the text, citations in the text with a bibliography, footnotes or endnotes – and you will be advised by your tutors, or in information from your subject department, which method is preferred. The information you use will be the same, whichever method you use, and you must be clear and consistent.

References or Citations in text

Some tutors like the full corresponding reference information to appear, in brackets, after each quote in an essay. This method has the advantage of making referencing easy and keeping all the information (quote and source) together but, it has the disadvantage of making the essay difficult to read.

The use of "citations" within the text of an essay, with an alphabetically arranged bibliography at the end, is the most commonly favoured method of referencing. This means that basic information about the source (author's surname, year of publication and page number) is given in brackets, following your quote, eg (MOLE, M. 2006. p.10), with the full reference appearing at the end of the essay. When using citations within the text, the full references in your bibliography should be listed in alphabetical order, not in the order in which the citations appear in the text.

Footnotes[4]

Footnotes are sometimes used for references if the essay is being typed. They have the advantage of keeping the reference information on the same sheet as the quote but some universities and colleges discourage their use because they can become clumsy and awkward to read if there are numerous quotes on a page.

Footnotes are formed by using the special "footnote" facility on your WP package. If you are not familiar with this function, check your on-screen help menu. The "footnote" facility will put a superscript (above the line) number in the position where you have placed your cursor to mark the end of your quote, it

---

[4] Do not confuse "footer" and "footnote". A "footer", like a "header", appears on every page of a document (e.g. an author's name, a chapter title or page numbers). A "footnote" appears at the foot of a single page and is relevant to something on that page.

will then take you to the bottom of the page so that you can write your reference there, for example[5].

When you have finished keying in your reference, just return your cursor to your main text and continue typing. When you type in your next quote, repeat the process[6].

Endnotes

Endnotes are similar to footnotes, except that the reference information is listed at the end of your essay. It is usual to have a separate section for references, starting on a new page, at the end of your essay.

If your WP package has an "endnote" facility (again, check the on-screen help menu), you can use it to insert a superscript number at the end of each quote and the relevant reference information at the end of the essay (providing you have your whole essay in one document). However, if you use this method, your references will not be listed in a new section at the end, but just after the end of the text.

If you use this method, and you want to separate your references from the text of your essay, you can simply insert a "page break" between the end of your essay and the endnotes. This will put your references onto a separate page. The endnote font size will be small (probably 10) so, to make it more easily

---

[5] this is where a footnote goes
[6] and your WP will give you the next number, and take you to the bottom of the page again to key in the next footnote

readable, you should highlight all of your references and increase the font size to 12.

To improve the appearance of your references, you should delete the endnote separator (using the help menu if necessary) and put an extra line space between each reference. Finally, put an underlined, bold heading: **References**, with an extra line space beneath it, at the top of the first page of your reference section.

If you want to use the endnote method of listing your references, but your WP package does not have an endnote facility, or you do not feel confident enough to use it, you can insert a superscript number yourself at the end of each quote or you can simply type the appropriate number, in brackets, after each consecutive quote in your essay, (for example "This is a quote in my essay"(1) or "This is another one"(2)) and then list your references, numbered and in the correct order, in their separate section at the end of your essay

The use of endnotes makes the essay easy to read, and presents the reference material in the same order as the quotes.

Separate reference and bibliography lists

If your full references appear as footnotes or endnotes, or if you put full references with your quotes in the text of your essay, then you might find it useful to have a separate bibliography. A bibliography is a list of other books, periodicals, etc which you have read while writing your essay.

You might not have quoted from these sources but listing them in this way gives your tutor information about the breadth of your research and gives you a reminder of books which have proved useful to you. It is not usually compulsory to have a separate bibliography.

If you have used citations in your text then you will list your full references in a bibliography at the end of your essay. In this case you can, if you choose, add to this list any other publications you have read while writing your essay.

ibid

If you have two consecutive quotes from the same page of the same publication, within your essay, you can simply write *ibid* for the second quote (whether you use a citation within the text, a footnote or an endnote). If the quotes are from the same publication, but from different pages, then you can write "*ibid* (p.xx)" (where xx is the page number of the second quote). *ibid* means "in the same place".

op cit

If you have several quotes from the same publication spread within your essay, then you should reference the first quote fully but subsequent references can be, eg. "*op cit* Mole, M. (2006)", with the page number of the quote. *op cit* means "in the work mentioned".

Now read the key points overleaf.

<u>REFERENCING – key points:</u>

- *Always* acknowledge the work of other people.

- Make sure that you know if there is a preferred style of referencing in your department.

- Make sure that every quote you have used is referenced with the correct corresponding reference information.

****

iv.   Presentation

The presentation of your work is very important. Good presentation will not necessarily earn extra marks but that is not because it is considered unimportant but, rather, because excellent presentation is expected at all times. You should, by now, have enough pride in your essay to want to match the hard work that you have put into its writing with a smart appearance for its submission.

At university or college you will be encouraged to prepare your essay for submission on a word-processor and, while it might be acceptable to submit neatly hand-written work, it is to your own advantage to try to learn WP skills. However good your hand-writing might be, it will deteriorate towards the end of copying-up an essay of several thousand words or when you are tired.

If you are not permitted to submit a hand-written essay, and you are not interested in developing WP skills, then it is likely that you will be able to find someone else to type your essay for you (for a fee).

There will probably be advertisements on student notice boards, or the administrative staff in your departmental office might know of freelance typists who provide such a service. However, you should remember that you will have to complete your essay well ahead of your submission deadline in order to give it to someone else to type and to collect it again for submission without exceeding your time limit. While the cost of having an essay typed for you is likely to be reasonable, the cost of having all of your essays typed for you during your course might exceed that of a laptop computer, particularly if you are doing a three- or four-year degree course. Think carefully about whether the cost of having your essays typed might cause you problems before you dismiss the idea of learning to use a WP package and bear in mind, too, that WP skills will be useful beyond education.

Your presentation should reflect the care you have taken with your essay. You will be doing a courtesy to your reader, and a favour to yourself, if you ensure that your work is clear and legible, and that all the relevant information is included. Your tutors are human beings and they will start to read a well presented essay in a better frame of mind than they would a piece of work submitted on scrappy, creased sheets of A4. Remember that they are busy and might have many essays to read and mark in a short space of time. Make it as easy for them as possible and give your essay the very best chance of achieving a really good grade. Your essay should have a front-sheet with all the information needed for its identification. For example:

(See overleaf)

Course number
or title

<u>ESSAY TITLE</u>

Your name
Date of submission

<u>(For *name of tutor*)</u>

(number of words)

If you are presenting statistics or charts in your essay, do make sure that they are clear and easily readable. Always label your x and y axes properly on graphs and, in any visual representation of data, remember to make your categories mutually exclusive.

The very simple fictitious charts on the next page show how poor labeling can cause confusion. Table 1 might indicate that there are quite dramatic fluctuations by age in the numbers of men or women watching TV news programmes but it would be of no use at all in trying to establish, for instance, how many 45 year old females do so, because the age of 45 could be read off from the second or the third column. Similarly, if we wanted to establish how many 30 year old males watched TV news programmes, we could read the percentage as 26.8 in column 1 (Age 18-30) but as 83.5 in column 2 (Age 30-45).

However, if the categories are re-labeled so that the age ranges are mutually exclusive, (as in Table 2), the chart becomes much more useful.

Table 2, with mutually exclusive categories, shows clearly into which categories a 30-year old male, or a 45 year old female, would fit.

See tables overleaf.

Table 1 Percentage of Adults watching TV news programmes

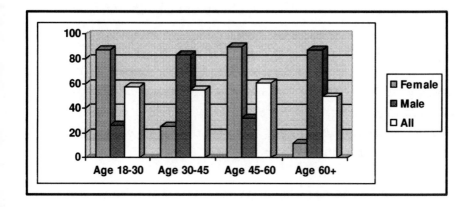

Table 2 Percentage of Adults watching TV news programmes

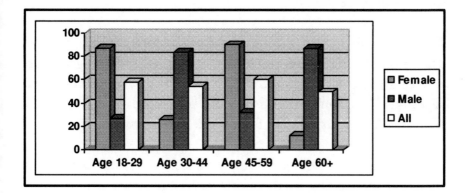

If you are submitting a hand-written essay, keep your writing as neat as possible. Leave an extra wide left-hand margin for your tutor's comments and write on alternate lines and one side of the sheet only. Use a black or blue pen or ballpoint.

Make sure you copy carefully from your draft and, if you make an error, correct it neatly. It is probably better to cross out neatly than to make a mess with correcting fluid. If you do use correcting fluid, make sure that it is not old or thick. Try to avoid marking the paper with your hand while you write. Remember to number your pages.

If you are typing the final copy of your essay, always use double line spacing and type on one side of the sheet only. Never use fancy fonts: Arial and Times New Roman are clear and will not distract your reader. Use an easily readable font-size - 12 is usually appropriate. Insert page numbers (using the on-screen help menu if necessary).

Remember to put an extra space (two in total) after a full stop and an extra line space between paragraphs. Indenting the first line of a paragraph (using the "tab" key) is now considered old-fashioned but some establishments still stipulate that it should be done. You must always follow the "house rules".

If you use sub-headings within your essay, ensure that you do not have a heading at the bottom of one page and then the relevant paragraph(s) on the next. You could just insert an extra line-space (or a page-break) above the sub-heading to move it onto the next page, with its text. However, if this leaves you with a large, unsightly gap at the foot of a page, then (if you are confident) you could:

- change the line-spacing of one or two paragraphs on that page to 1.5 so that the sub-heading fits on to the page with the first two lines of the following paragraph

- change that page to font size 14, to reduce the gap at the bottom of the page

- place an extra line space before the first line at the top of the page

Any of these solutions must *only* be used on the final version of your essay. If you used any of them, and then did some more editing and deleted or moved text, then you could be left with a worse problem than the separated sub-heading and text with which you started!

Your Reference and/or Bibliography sections should always start on new sheets with a clear heading. Use single line spacing for these sections, with an extra line-space between the entries.

If you used citations within your text, then you will only need one, combined, References and Bibliography section. If you used the endnote method then all your references will be in the order in which they appear in your essay, and you might choose to have a separate bibliography section.

If you have any appendices, these are placed at the end of the essay, before the references and bibliography sections, and are traditionally numbered using Roman numerals (e.g. Appendix I, Appendix II, etc).

Always keep a printed copy of your essay, as well as saving it on disk, at least until the submitted copy has been marked and returned to you. It is unlikely that anything will go wrong but, if an essay became mislaid or damaged by accident, it would not be such a disaster if there was another copy to hand, ready to be submitted in its place.

When you have finished printing your essay and you have all the pages together (and in the correct order), including references, bibliography and any appendices, you should either staple them together or, even better, put them into a plastic folder. Do not use clear plastic pockets when submitting essays. Tutors who mark many essays during the course of a term do not want to have to spend time taking each one out of a pocket before starting to read it. If you use a plastic folder, you can transfer your essay to a pocket or a ring binder when it is returned to you (ready to use for revision later in the academic year) and use the folder to submit another essay. Plastic folders are almost endlessly reusable and will give a final sparkle to your well written, well presented piece of work.

Your departmental office will have an established routine for the submission of essays and you should follow that. Make sure, in advance, that you know if you should be submitting your work in duplicate. Do you need to obtain a receipt when you submit? If so, is there a special form you should prepare in advance?

You must submit your essay by the deadline you have been given unless you have an extremely good reason to ask for an extension. At some establishments, individual tutors do not have the authority to grant extensions and, if you think your circumstances are such that you deserve one, then you will need to ask somebody higher up the academic ladder and you will need to have a very good reason indeed for making your request.

In any event, it is unfair to request extra time unless there really are extenuating circumstances. Other students will have worked very hard to complete and submit their essay on time and will not look kindly on your being granted an extension – with an extra week, everyone could probably have written a better essay, why should you be the only one granted the privilege of more time? Also, for you, submitting an essay a week or fortnight late means that you have that week or fortnight less to work on the next piece of work due for submission. By the end of the term you will be well behind with your work and struggling to catch up. If you do have a genuine reason to ask for more time, then you will be treated sympathetically. If not, then you must submit to the deadline, like everybody else.

By the time you finally submit your essay, it will seem very familiar to you because you will have put a good deal of effort into its preparation. This means that you might now read it and think it is so many pages of puerile rubbish or you might think it is a modern masterpiece which will leave your tutors awe-struck. It is likely to be neither. Your essay will fall between those extremes but, for now, there is nothing you can do but wait for its return.

Take some time to relax and unwind a little – before you start your next essay.

<u>Now read the key points overleaf.</u>

<u>PRESENTATION – key points:</u>

- Present your work as neatly and attractively as possible

- Submit your essay on or before the due date

- RELAX

****

v.   Afterwards

When your essay is returned to you, marked and commented upon by your tutor, there will be some anxious moments as you look for the mark and (probably later) as you read her or his comments.

It is always good to be given a grade that corresponds with the amount of time and effort you have lavished on your essay and one that mirrors your own assessment of the standard of your work. However, essay marking is subjective and this does not always happen.

You will have acquired a considerable amount of knowledge about your essay subject while you have been researching and writing; you will also have learnt how to work constructively and you will have improved the way you express yourself in writing. Now is the time to learn from your tutor's opinion of your essay.

While the mark you have been given is important (especially if it counts towards your course result), your tutor's comments should also always be regarded as valuable. Do take the time to read these comments. Some will be positive some might be critical but, hopefully, always constructive. Remember that your tutor knows and understands the subject you are studying and if any errors in your understanding or interpretation of your research are pointed out to you, then you should accept the advice and act upon it, if appropriate, in subsequent essays.

If there are comments on your essay about your writing style, the breadth of your research, or how you might improve your work in future, do consider these carefully. They have not been written to upset or undermine you, they have been written to help. If it does happen to you, remember that your tutor has taken the trouble to make the comments, it would be courteous of you to take the trouble to read them.

The protocol around returning essays varies quite widely. Your essay might be returned to you, with written comments, via your pigeonhole or your tutor might hand it to you personally during a lecture. Alternatively, you might be invited for a tutorial which will give you the chance to discuss the mark you have been given and your tutor's comments.

If your tutor has commented in writing and, having read the comments carefully, you feel that they need further clarification, then you should ask to see your tutor to discuss the matter. Similarly if, having noted the comments, you feel that either the mark you have been given, or the comments that have been made, are unfair then you should see your tutor.

If, having discussed the matter fully with your tutor, you are still dissatisfied with your mark, then it might be possible to request a "re-mark". This would mean that you would have to submit your essay to another tutor who would disregard the first mark and assess it again. If this is an option for you, and you decide to take it up, then it is considered courteous to inform the tutor who first marked your essay that you are requesting a re-mark. She or he should receive this information in a professional manner. You should remember that, when re-assessed, your mark can go down as well as up.

<u>AFTERWARDS – key points:</u>

- Always carefully consider your tutor's comments on your essay

- If you do not understand the comments, discuss them with your tutor

- If you are dissatisfied with your mark, discuss this with your tutor

- Learn from your essay

****

<u>Appendix</u>
SAMPLE ESSAY PLAN

<u>EXAMPLE of "preliminary questions" to stimulate thinking for an essay plan:</u>

In planning this genuine, first-year undergraduate essay, entitled:

<u>"Discuss the advantages and disadvantages of retrospective evidence"*</u>

the writer asked the following preliminary questions:

- What do we mean by retrospective evidence?

- Why do we use it?

- What are the advantages? for whom? who says so?

- What are the disadvantages? for whom? who says so?

- What do we conclude? do advantages outweigh disadvantages?

Having given some thought to the answers to the preliminary questions, a suitable introduction might begin with:

> "In attempting to answer the question and identify the advantages and disadvantages of retrospective evidence

118

it is helpful to look at why we use retrospective evidence at all. If we want information about the past there are always history books to be consulted, past copies of magazines and newspapers relating to the period of interest and now, of course, recordings of radio programmes from which we may glean information on almost any aspect of any period over the last sixty or seventy years. However, these seldom show life from the perspective of individuals and almost never from the perspective of working class people whose lives were considered to be unworthy of serious consideration until after a majority labour government was returned in 1945, leading to the working classes being recognised as more than just comic caricatures.

Retrospective evidence (for the purposes of this paper I shall consider "retrospective evidence" to mean retrospective *oral* evidence), goes some way towards redressing this imbalance of history. The spoken memories of individuals can give us vital, previously un-noted, information about internal family life, marriage, raising children etc, which, in turn, can indicate changes or similarities in personal relationship patterns and attitudes over the years"

With just a few more sentences to expand on the use of retrospective oral evidence, supported by quotes, the writer is then ready to lead into the main body of the essay with some "signposting":

"Having briefly established the utility of retrospective evidence in helping to view history from a personal, individual perspective, I will attempt to identify the advantages and disadvantages. I believe that there are advantages and disadvantages on both sides, (i.e. for the researcher and for the informant) and in this paper I will try to show the reasons for this belief."

In this introduction the writer has examined the phrase "retrospective evidence" (retrospective evidence is the memories of individuals, spoken in their own words); clarified how s/he intends to interpret the question (by considering "retrospective evidence" to mean retrospective *oral* evidence), outlined the reasons for its use (to give us information about the every-day life of those whose experiences are not recorded in history books) and said what s/he is going to do in this essay ("I will attempt to identify the advantages and disadvantages ….. on both sides").

Having written a strong introduction, the writer can then lead easily into the main body of the essay, and look at:

- the advantages of retrospective oral evidence (ROE) in general – what society gains: a different, valid perspective on history; the opportunity to put history into context; qualitative material to complement statistics, written documents etc.
- the disadvantages in general: ROE is subjective; the information volunteered is not "reliable" (in a scientific

sense); it is an individual's testimony and cannot be considered representative.

- the advantages for the informant: ROE emphasises the value of an individual's life; improves the quality of life; gives the informant status.

- the disadvantages for the informant: giving ROE might bring back unhappy memories or feelings.

- the advantages for the researcher: satisfaction of introducing to history people who have not been heard before; deeper understanding of history; opportunity to build up a previously unseen "picture" which will complement quantitative studies and make history more democratic.

- the disadvantages for the researcher: collecting ROE requires more thorough preparation than other forms of research; care must be taken to avoid "selecting" parts of the evidence given by informants which support researcher's own prejudices. The researcher needs a great deal of sensitivity when interacting with individuals but must remain objective when assembling the evidence of several (or more) informants for a final study.

Answers to the preliminary questions form a strong foundation for the body of an essay which looks at, and answers, the question raised in the essay title. With the responses to our preliminary questions expanded into paragraphs, and quotes inserted to support the points made, the body of the essay is written and all that is now needed is a brief concluding paragraph.

In a first year, undergraduate essay, a single paragraph would be enough to conclude the essay. For example:

> "Having examined the major advantages and disadvantages of retrospective evidence, it could be concluded that ....."

****

www.straightforwardco.co.uk

All titles, listed below, in the Straightforward Guides Series can be purchased online, using credit card or other forms of payment by going to www.straightfowardco.co.uk A discount of 25% per title is offered with online purchases.

Law

A Straightforward Guide to:
Consumer Rights
Bankruptcy Insolvency and the Law
Employment Law
Private Tenants Rights
Family law
Small Claims in the County Court
Contract law
Intellectual Property and the law
Divorce and the law
Leaseholders Rights
The Process of Conveyancing
Knowing Your Rights and Using the Courts
Producing Your own Will
Housing Rights
The Bailiff the law and You
Probate and The Law
Company law
What to Expect When You Go to Court
Guide to Competition Law
Give me Your Money-Guide to Effective Debt Collection
Caring for a Disabled Child

<u>General titles</u>

Letting Property for Profit
Buying, Selling and Renting property
Buying a Home in England and France
Bookkeeping and Accounts for Small Business

Creative Writing
Freelance Writing
Writing Your own Life Story
Writing performance Poetry
Writing Romantic Fiction
Speech Writing

Teaching Your Child to Read and write
Teaching Your Child to Swim
Raising a Child-The Early Years

Creating a Successful Commercial Website
The Straightforward Business Plan
The Straightforward C.V.
Successful Public Speaking

Handling Bereavement
Play the Game-A Compendium of Rules
Individual and Personal Finance
Understanding Mental Illness

The Two Minute Message
Guide to Self Defence

Buying a Used Car
Tiling for Beginners

Go to:

www.straightforwardco.co.uk